Simon Gray was born in 1936 in Hayling Island.
He lives in London with his wife, two cats and a dog.

by the same author

non-fiction
AN UNNATURAL PURSUIT
HOW'S THAT FOR TELLING 'EM, FAT LADY?
ENTER A FOX
FAT CHANCE
THE SMOKING DIARIES

fiction
COLMAIN
SIMPLE PEOPLE
LITTLE PORTIA
A COMEBACK FOR STARK
BREAKING HEARTS

stage plays
WISE CHILD, MOLLY, SPOILED, DUTCH UNCLE,
THE IDIOT (adaptation), DOG DAYS, THE REAR COLUMN,
STAGE STRUCK, THE COMMON PURSUIT, MELON,
HIDDEN LAUGHTER, THE HOLY TERROR, CELL MATES,
SIMPLY DISCONNECTED, LIFE SUPPORT

SIMON GRAY: KEY PLAYS
(*Butley, Otherwise Engaged, Close of Play,
Quartermaine's Terms, The Late Middle Classes*)

SIMON GRAY: FOUR PLAYS
(*The Pig Trade, Japes Too, Michael, The Holy Terror*)

published by Nick Hern Books
JUST THE THREE OF US, JAPES, THE LATE MIDDLE CLASSES

television plays
THE CARAMEL CRISIS, DEATH OF A TEDDY BEAR,
AWAY WITH THE LADIES, SLEEPING DOG,
SPOILED, PIG IN A POKE, MAN IN A SIDE-CAR,
PLAINTIFFS AND DEFENDANTS, TWO SUNDAYS,
FEMME FATALE, RUNNING LATE, UNNATURAL PURSUITS

television films
AFTER PILKINGTON, OLD FLAMES,
THEY NEVER SLEPT, THE COMMON PURSUIT

films
A MONTH IN THE COUNTRY

SIMON GRAY

The Old Masters

faber and faber

First published in 2004
by Faber and Faber Limited
3 Queen Square, London WC1N 3AU

Reprinted with revisions 2004

Typeset by Country Setting, Kingsdown, Kent CT14 8ES
Printed in England by Intype London Ltd

All rights reserved
© Simon Gray, 2004

The right of Simon Gray to be identified as author
of this work has been asserted in accordance with Section 77
of the Copyright, Designs and Patents Act 1988

All rights whatsoever in this work are strictly reserved.
Applications for permission for any use whatsoever,
including performance rights, must be made in advance,
prior to any such proposed use, to Judy Daish Associates,
2 St Charles Place, London W10 6EG.
For English-speaking amateur rights (excluding
the USA and Canada), apply to Samuel French Limited,
52 Fitzroy Street, London W1T 5JR. No performance
may be given unless a licence has first been obtained.

This book is sold subject to the condition that it shall not,
by way of trade or otherwise, be lent, resold, hired out
or otherwise circulated without the publisher's prior consent
in any form of binding or cover other than that in which
it is published and without a similar condition including
this condition being imposed on the subsequent purchaser

A CIP record for this book
is available from the British Library

0-571-22765-1

2 4 6 8 10 9 7 5 3 1

Alan Bates
(1934–2003)

The Old Masters was first presented at Birmingham Repertory Theatre on 4 June 2003, and transferred to the Comedy Theatre, London, on 1 July 2004. The cast was as follows:

BB Edward Fox
Mary Barbara Jefford
Nicky Sally Dexter
Fowles Steven Pacey
Duveen Peter Bowles

Directed by Harold Pinter
Designed by Eileen Diss
Costumes by Dany Everett
Lighting by Mick Hughes
Sound by John Leonard, for Aura Sound

Characters

BB
Mary
Nicky
Fowles
Duveen

Act One

SCENE ONE

Garden of Villa I Tatti, 1937. A lovely evening, about seven o'clock. Mary is seated in garden, reading a letter. There is a bottle of wine in an ice bucket. Three glasses. She is sipping a glass of wine. Sound of voices, a man's and a woman's. Mary looks up, picks up the letter, puts the letter under the others, as if concealing it, hurriedly pours herself a glass, settles into what looks like a dozing position.

BB enters, with Nicky. BB in late forties, Nicky a little younger.

BB is in full flow, to Nicky.

BB – and that soon the Duck will imitate him as he imitates him in everything else, but with a dash of Italian originality – black shirts instead of brown shirts, this (*imitating Fascist salute*) instead of that (*imitating Nazi salute*) – quack quack quack, instead of heil, heil, heil! But which is which? And does it matter? Quack, heil, heil, quack – (*giving alternate salutes*) – quack, heil.

Mary I do wish you wouldn't do that. The servants might see you, and we don't know their politics.

BB Perhaps it's time we found out.

Mary Whatever they might think about Signor Mussolini, he is not the duck. He is Il Duce, the head of their government. They might not care to have him mocked by a guest of the country. Hasn't it occurred to you that they could get into trouble for not reporting your antics to the police? We have no idea what risks they might be running simply by being members of the household.

BB turns away, pours himself some wine.

BB Your point is taken. They are good to us and we should respect their feelings. I shall quack *sotto voce* in future.

Nicky You've been looking at the bills, Mary?

BB The bills? Why?

Mary I didn't intend to open them but, once I started, I couldn't stop – like smoking or eating chocolates. (*to Nicky*) Can we really pay them all?

Nicky Well, they shouldn't be very different from last month's, so we'll probably manage.

Mary Probably! What do you mean, 'probably'? What does she mean?

BB She means, of course, that we shall pay them as always on time and in full. Is there anything for me? (*noticing letter*) Who is that from? (*making to pick it up*) I recognise the handwriting.

Mary (*lurches away from Nicky, snatches it up*) It's from Karin. (*Sits down, stares defiantly up at BB.*) She's coming to stay.

BB When?

Mary The week after next.

BB For how long?

Mary She doesn't really say.

BB What do you mean – you can't be saying that she's written to you informing you that she intends to impose herself on me for an unknown period – you invited her! Why?

Mary Perhaps because she's my daughter, and I'd like to see her. Also she needs a holiday –

BB From her husband I suppose. (*Gestures.*) An abominable little man. I believe I can say that without giving offence, as he's not a blood relative, my dear. Actually I'm quite fond of Karin, especially when she's not obliged to play the besieged wife and mother.

Mary She'll be playing the besieged grandmother.

BB She's bringing those children, all those children –!

Mary The children are all in their twenties, as you know perfectly well. She's bringing her only grandchild, little Roger, who is very quiet and likes to read. I believe you're confusing Karin with Rachel. Probably quite deliberately.

BB No, not quite deliberately. Your daughters, their children, are confusing in themselves, I do nothing deliberately to confuse them, they – they – well, I shall not be here to entertain them. I shall go away for this unknown period, Nicky will accompany me, of course. Please make arrangements, Nicky. Book us first to Paris, then to London, we shall treat ourselves to a suite in the Ritz of both towns, you shall travel as Mrs Berenson, to save embarrassment, and to keep the expenses down. Go now. Do it at once.

Mary (*reaching out her arm for Nicky's support, as she goes back to her chair*) Oh, really, BB, really, really, really – you hate my family because you're jealous of them.

BB What, of the attention you give them, is that what you believe?

Mary No, it's not what I believe. You're jealous of them for being my children.

BB (*to Nicky*) I'm quarrelling with my wife and you're still here. Should you be?

Mary Yes, you should be, so don't you dare – and don't you dare, BB, my family is my family – this is my home, I will ask them here. I will ask them here! (*She is clearly upset.*)

There is a pause, as Mary and BB look at each other.

BB Of course, of course, my dear. And I will make them welcome as always. I was only being irritable. Though I like to think that we too, the ones already in your home, are also your family. (*Goes to her, kisses her on the cheek.*) Now I must go and do some work – Fowles will be arriving at any minute.

Mary No, he won't.

BB What? What do you mean?

Mary He's already here. I forgot about him because you've driven him out of my mind with all your – your –

BB Where is he, then?

Mary I sent him to have a little rest. Had a very bad journey, some trouble – yes, some trouble with the trains. And there's something else I've forgotten, BB. Your Swedish girl won't be up this evening, to do your massage. Apparently she has to be somewhere at seven, an emergency.

BB An emergency. She has to give an emergency massage?

Mary Probably someone needs her for something serious.

Nicky She looks after the footballers in Florence, she told me.

Mary Does she? I didn't know that. Well, there you are, BB, this evening you give way to the footballers of Florence. How many are there in a team of footballers?

Nicky Oh, twelve, I think. Twelve or thirteen.

Mary Twelve or thirteen! No wonder she won't be up to you this evening, poor thing!

BB Quack, quack, quack. When Fowles wakes, tell him I shall be in the library. (*Goes in.*)

Mary There. I got my own back. I know. I know. I should be nicer. But then so should he.

Nicky I don't think you should be nicer – I think he needs you to be like this, at the moment.

Mary Besides, you're nice enough for the both of us. (*Takes her hand.*) I mean that nicely.

Nicky Well – I sometimes wish I weren't.

Mary But you don't mind about the little Swedish thing, do you?

Nicky Of course I do. Did you tell her not to come?

Mary No, I'm afraid I didn't. I wouldn't dare.

Nicky So she'll be back tomorrow, will she?

Mary I expect so. Unless you find a way of stopping her.

Nicky I wouldn't dare.

Mary You could if you wanted. You have all the weapons, after all. He needs you, my dear.

Nicky Much less than he needs you.

Mary Oh, let's not get into one of those conversations, it always ends with our deciding that he needs us both, though I can never remember quite what it is that he needs me for. If you're not going to put your foot down, you'll have to accept her as one of the penalties of loving an unfaithful man with an appetite. And you know – much better a Swedish masseuse than something Italian. No emotional nonsense from her –

Nicky No, only from him, when she doesn't show up. He's such a child.

Mary Perhaps all very exceptional men are. Or so women in our position usually claim.

Nicky Yes. (*Laughs.*) I suppose we do. Well, I'd better deal with these bills. (*Picking up bills, moves to go off.*)

Mary Yes, it's very bad, isn't it?

Nicky No, really, we'll manage.

Mary (*to herself*) Bad, bad, very bad –

Thinking Nicky's gone, she puts her head back, then her hand to her stomach, clearly in pain. Nicky sees, goes across to her, puts her hand on Mary's forehead.

Why do you always do that, when I never have a temperature? (*Takes Nicky's hand away, gently holds it.*)

Nicky But you have. I felt it. The doctor is coming tomorrow.

Mary I don't think I need him.

Nicky Yes, you do.

Mary Very well then, I don't think I want him. I only have one objective at the moment – to keep going just as I am until Karin and little Roger have visited.

Nicky But that's not for another two weeks, you said. And – and why not see the doctor so that you're at your best for them?

Mary This is my best! (*sharply*) Now leave me alone, there's a good girl!

As Nicky makes to withdraw her hand, Mary grabs it.

I'm sorry, my dear, sorry for being an old – old – you see, you see, something's happening to me, it seems to be growing in here – (*Gestures to stomach.*) – like my illness, as part of my illness, it's fear for my children, dread, they're so hopeless with money, they never seem able to manage even with what I send them – so how can they survive if the war comes and we lose everything, and I have nothing – nothing to send?

Nicky But you know, Mary, the war hasn't come. Things might get better. Mr Fowles may have brought us the money Joe owes BB –

Mary It won't be enough.

Nicky Let me.

Mary Oh, if only BB would let Joe come here himself and be our friend again. He would find a way of helping, Joe could always pull something out of the hat when we most needed it. Little Fowles, he's very sweet I know, and tries to be helpful, but there's something about him I don't quite – of course he used to be Joe's lift-boy, you know, taking people up and down in the lift from Joe's office, listening to their conversations, then reporting back to Joe – a sort of infant sneak. Well, actually I hope he's still a bit of a sneak, in fact I'm counting on it.

Nicky You told him something you want him to report back to Joe?

Mary I trust he will. Joe has children, he dotes on his grandchild, he will understand why I am so worried. I only told Fowles what I've just told you – But the message should be quite clear – please, Joe, help me.

Nicky But wouldn't it have been better to write direct to Joe?

Mary I couldn't take the risk. It would have been evidence of treachery, BB would call it, treachery, so you see nothing may come of it.

Fowles appears, carrying a picture, wrapped, and a case containing files. He is not yet seen by Mary and Nicky and hears the following.

Fowles may forget to pass it on, may think it's an old lady's ramblings. I thought of bribing him, he may still just be a lift-boy at heart, with a habit of tips and bribes, perhaps Joe encourages it.

Nicky (*seeing Fowles, warningly*) Oh, Mr Fowles.

Mary Ah, there you are, Mr Fowles, you're here, good.

Fowles Yes, here I am. (*putting picture down*) Miss Mariano. (*Goes over, shakes her hand.*)

Nicky Mr Fowles.

Mary And did you manage a little sleep, Mr Fowles?

Fowles Actually, I sat at the window, looking out – couldn't resist – one of my favourite views, you know. And the light!

Mary Yes, the light! (*She attempts to struggle to her feet. The extent of her drinking is now clear.*) The light! I think it's time I had a little less of it, myself.

Fowles (*going tentatively towards her*) Can I give you a –

Mary No, no, I can manage. (*Moves towards the house. Stops, without turning.*) Mr Fowles, you overheard me saying things I wish I hadn't said. Or rather, that I wish you hadn't heard.

Fowles Oh, no, no, Mrs Berenson, I was very glad to overhear the little I did, it makes things – well, easier when one understands the situation. People's feelings. They often don't make them clear enough. A great help. And I haven't forgotten our conversation. I'd be glad to give you any help I can by mentioning it to Joe, but simply as a conversation between you and me. I am grateful to you for not offering a tip or bribe. It might have prevented me from performing a friendly service for you, by making it seem something else, and that would have been a pity.

Mary (*turns her head, smiles*) That is very gentlemanly, Mr Fowles. I am ashamed of myself. Perhaps one day when you have grandchildren –

Fowles I hope I will care for them as you care for yours.

Mary Thank you. (*going off*) And I think I forgot to ask earlier – the boy is still doing well, is he, at school?

Fowles Still doing well, thank you for asking.

Mary goes off.

Nicky Both still doing well, I hope?

Fowles Yes. David's turning into a little classicist.

Nicky You could probably do with a glass of wine?

Fowles Yes, I could. But I won't. I'm trying not to drink except with meals. If that's all right.

Nicky It's perfectly all right.

Fowles And how is –?

Nicky I'm to tell you he's in the library. You had a bad journey – some trouble on the train, wasn't there?

Fowles Oh, yes. Immigration officers, they said they were, but probably the police, really, looking for spies. Took me for a spy – and then they saw his name on one of my papers. Duveen, they said, Joseph Duveen, your employer is a Jew – and Berenson, you are going to visit a Signor Bernard Berenson, also a Jew, possibly? It was all like that, and I kept saying that Mr Duveen was an Anglo-American, I kept stressing American. Joe would have hated that, you know how important being English is to him, especially in America, but now in Italy I've made him into an Anglo-*American* businessman and art lover with a special love of the great Italian artists, and Mr Berenson the world's greatest expert on the great Italian artists – they both worshipped Italy for her history, her beauty, her people, that's what they were, who they were, neither of them in the slightest sense Jewish in the important sense of the word, etc., etc. – but it was all very shameful, especially if I think of the times I congratulated them on all the splendid changes taking place all around us, how wonderfully punctual the train was, going through stations to the minute, how I wished our English trains – it's the atmosphere, the arrogance and brutish stupidity, even my usual hotel in Florence – not – not Italian, really. Not my dear old Italy, eh?

Nicky No. I expect you must be anxious to be away, back to London.

Fowles Oh, well – it's pleasant enough to be here, in the garden.

Nicky No danger in it.

Fowles There's always a touch of danger at I Tatti.

Nicky Even here? With me?

Fowles Ah.

Nicky Ah? A diplomatic ah.

Fowles Sometimes especially even with you, Miss Mariano. A touch of danger.

Nicky If there is, it's you who bring it to me, Mr Fowles.

Fowles I was talking about how very – how very charming you always look – that sort of danger.

Nicky Thank you. But you are safe. (*Smiles prettily.*) Am I?

Fowles Well, there is a little thing – not exactly dangerous, of course not. But it depends on whether I stay on to dinner or not. I'm expected, am I?

Nicky Of course. You always stay to dinner.

Fowles Well, if I do, you won't have to do anything, because it'll mean I think I've got a chance of persuading BB to do what Joe wants him to do. But if I don't manage it, if things are going badly, I won't stay to dinner. You see? And Joe will take over.

Nicky Joe? You mean he's here, he's actually here?

Fowles Yes. Well, in Florence. He's come specially to see BB. If I fail, that is. As a last resort.

Nicky I don't think BB will want to see him.

Fowles Perhaps not, but he thinks that all he needs is someone to open the door for him, you see, so he isn't turned away before he has his chance. Once he's actually in front of BB and gets going – well, you know Joe. He believes completely in his power to charm. Even BB.

Nicky And he's right. He gets BB to play with him, and BB hates him for it immediately afterwards. Really, it's a bit like a bad love affair.

Fowles laughs, rather coarsely, stops himself.

Fowles That's an – a very interesting way of putting it.

Nicky He should come after Mary has gone to bed. She adores him, of course, and BB hates seeing them together, it makes him jealous – though I'm never sure which one he's jealous of. Perhaps he isn't, either.

Fowles laughs again, slightly.

Nicky She's never up much past nine. Tell him to come at ten o'clock sharp, and to ring very lightly, so as not to wake her.

Fowles Ten o'clock sharp.

Nicky I'll be waiting by the door. (*Smiles.*) But of course I'd much prefer it if you stayed for dinner.

Fowles So would Joe, I expect.

Nicky May I ask what it is that Joe wants, precisely? That's so important that he'll risk wasting a journey – and BB's insults?

Fowles He wants him to change his mind about an attribution.

Nicky Oh. The Masaccio that Mellon bought –

Fowles No, no. Nothing to do with the Masaccio, but the one Joe really wants him to – to think again about is a Titian. A Giorgione, rather. From Giorgione to Titian. No, I mean the other way around. Sorry. Titian to Gior – (*Gestures.*) You see. The mere thought of talking to BB about it makes me flustered –

Nicky It must be *The Adoration of the Shepherds*.

Fowles Yes. That's the one. What do you think of my chances?

Nicky I think I hope the food is good in your hotel.

Fowles And what about Joe's chances?

Nicky Ah well, Joe is Joe. It might depend on what he has to offer.

Fowles I'll tell him that.

Nicky I expect he already knows.

Fowles Yes. Well, well – I suppose I'd better be off to the library, and try my luck. Thank you, Miss Mariano, for all your usual – kindness. (*Takes her hand.*) I do enjoy our little –

Nicky Trysts.

Fowles Yes, well, I don't flatter myself, our little business meetings – Oh. (*Little pause, slightly embarrassed.*) There's something for – from Joe, a little token of his gratitude (*fumbling in his pocket*). To add to your collection. He came across it in Boston apparently. (*Takes out a small box. Is about to hand it to Nicky.*)

BB enters.

BB Oh, here you are. (*to Fowles*) I hope you've had a decent rest. You seem to have had a long one. I've been waiting quite a time.

Fowles Sorry, BB. (*slipping box back into his pocket*) I was just sorting out with Miss Mariano some things, details – so that I won't need to trouble you with them.

BB The detail of a certain Italian count, perhaps?

He goes to wine bucket, pours himself a glass of wine, sees Fowles's glass, comes over, fills it with wine, offers some to Nicky, who refuses.

Fowles What?

BB Joe recently wrote asking me whether the rumour is true that I've been keeping company with the gentleman.

Nicky (*to Fowles*) Gianisanti. Il Conte di Gianisanti.

Fowles Oh. Oh yes.

BB As I haven't bothered to reply I assume he's put you on to the case.

Fowles Yes, well, yes – as a matter of fact he did ask me to ask you whether you'd been advising the Count about the value of some paintings in his collection.

BB And if I have?

Fowles Well, Joe just wanted me to remind you that he has an exclusive contract with you.

BB A contract has to be honoured on both sides, does it not?

Fowles In what respect do you think that Joe has failed to honour?

BB Well, only on the money front, perhaps? As his *employee* I note that my wages are on an unusual course – as the years pass, they diminish. (*to Nicky*) Remind me, my dear girl, what my wages were in 1927?

Nicky In the region of fifty thousand dollars.

BB And now, ten years later?

Nicky Twenty thousand dollars.

BB From fifty to twenty – and so next year – given that we're still alive next year, and not in captivity to the duck – what can we expect next year, if this rate of decline continues? Ten thousand, five thousand – and he complains because I seek for other sources – no, not seek, I don't seek other sources, other sources seek me.

After all, who else can they turn to? And what can I do under the circumstances, speaking as a man who is likely to have descended from fifty to five?

Fowles Well, the thing is, BB, if you'll excuse me, but the fact is that the market is the market, and percentages are percentages, and that's what your contract with Joe deals in – when Joe's income drops your percentage remains the same but your income drops too, in proportion as Joe's drops. It's worth remembering, BB, if I may say so, that while other men were throwing themselves out of windows on Wall Street, Joe not only survived but kept you on as much as twenty thousand dollars a year. Furthermore there's every reason to believe that we may soon start climbing back to where we were, war or no war, and your income would rise in proportion – depending, of course, on contracts being – well – contracts.

BB Very well, Edward, I'll accept that. Tell him, my dear, about the nature of my dealings with the Conte di Gianisanti. Miss Mariano accompanied me.

Nicky We paid him a visit in Milan, you looked at some of his paintings, he asked for your advice.

BB Which –?

Nicky You withheld. You explained that you were exclusively consultant to Joe.

Fowles Ah.

BB For the while. I decided to wait for your visit. Either that or a cheque. A cheque – I mean you no discourtesy – would have been preferable. (*Little pause.*) As there is still money outstanding, I believe, is there not, my dear?

Nicky Eighteen and a half thousand pounds.

Fowles Yes. Well, then – I'll ask Joe to settle it as soon as I get back.

BB And?

Fowles And it'll be settled.

BB There. (*to Nicky*) You've heard that. Marked the time and the date.

Nicky uses Mary's pen and paper to write it quickly. BB takes both from her, hands them to Fowles.

Fowles I'm sorry you think there's a need for this.

BB So am I.

Fowles And the Count in Milan?

BB The relationship will cease, you have my word on it.

Fowles (*handing pen and paper back to Nicky*) Your word?

BB Indeed.

Fowles Well, that will do for Joe, I'm sure.

BB (*pours more wine into Fowles's glass*) I'm relieved to hear it. (*spotting package*) And what is that?

Fowles It's the copy you asked for. I've done it. The Tacconi. (*picking up package*)

BB (*clearly at a loss*) You've done it?

Fowles Well, I mean, had it done. Picked it up from Mme Helfer on my way through Paris. Here. See what you think. (*Begins to open package.*)

BB (*recognising contents*) No, wait, it can wait –

Nicky looks at the painting, now free of paper.

Nicky Oh. Yes, of course. (*clearly upset*) So here it is. She's done it beautifully, as usual, Mme Helfer. If it is the copy. Are you sure it is? She's been so quick –

Fowles What? (*anxiously*) Well, surely she wouldn't have got them muddled –

BB (*almost snatching picture from Nicky, stares at it*) Of course it's the copy. She's almost a genius, Mme Helfer, but look – here – and here – slightest thinness – almost a signature for almost a genius, but a copier cannot be a genius, it's a contradiction – I'm sure Mary needs you, Nicky, shouldn't you go to her, please.

Nicky (*to Fowles, collecting paper and letters*) I'll see you at dinner, Mr Fowles, I trust.

Fowles Well – (*Gestures ambiguously.*)

Nicky goes off.

BB I did ask you – I believe I did ask you – to keep this private.

Fowles Well, yes, but I didn't think that included – I'm very sorry, it really didn't occur to me –

BB When I say private I mean, from the women. Otherwise I don't bother to use the word, as I assume that every detail of our business together is kept private from the world.

Fowles I see. Well, it's never come up before. I'll remember it in future, BB, but she seemed to know about it anyway –

BB Yes, yes – it's her feelings, her feelings – Mary's too – well, mine, I admit, mine too. I'm not easy about it, and they both sense it, and that makes me even less easy.

Fowles But it's for a good cause, isn't it, for some sick men in one of the villages, they'll be getting a bit of money for treatment now, from the sale of the original –

BB Yes.

Fowles Well, then.

BB Not men, boys still. Boys sent by the duck to Abyssinia, poisoned by the duck's own gas. Their priest took us to meet them, we saw for ourselves what it had done to them – and then he took us into his church and showed us what was hanging behind the altar – I could scarcely believe my eyes, but as my eyes never lie, even in the gloom of an unlit church, so – so the priest and I made a deal. And his church will now have this – (*Gestures to painting.*) – hanging behind his altar.

Fowles But no one else will know the difference, that's all that matters, isn't it? You should see yourself as providence, God's instrument, that kind of thing. What is there to be ashamed of, BB? The people will think they're looking at the painting they've always looked at, the priest will be able to get treatment for those poor lads –

BB – and Joe and I will make a considerable sum of money.

Fowles A good deed isn't the less a good deed because everybody benefits. And it won't be that large a sum. At least, all the bids Joe's had so far have been less than he expected.

BB Well, that makes me feel much better. Thank you. Tell him if he can't get a decent bid – a decent bid – I'll find someone else who will.

Fowles Oh, I'm sure he'll get a decent bid. The lads will get their treatment, don't worry, BB.

BB looks at him suspiciously.

And we'll get our profit, don't worry, BB. (*Little pause.*) Oh. There are some photographs – (*reaching into his pocket*) – he wants you to look at. (*Hands them to BB.*)

BB (*shuffles through them, giving each a fierce scrutiny*) A student's portfolio. School of Pesellino, School of Sebastiano, School of Baldovinetti, school of, school of – we have nothing of value here. What is this, this, what is this?

Fowles (*looks at photograph*) Well, that's the Bellini, isn't it, Joe's had it cleaned.

BB Cleaned, cleaned, he's had it defiled . . . Defiled!

Fowles Well, you know the Americans, they like their masterpieces to look as fresh as paint.

BB I haven't seen it, I haven't seen it, make sure I haven't seen it or I shall have to speak about what I've seen. (*Little pause.*) How ghastly this all is, how ghastly!

Fowles Sorry, BB?

BB Nothing, nothing, I – was addressing myself.

Fowles Oh. Can I say, may I just say – I know how you must feel, sometimes, it's difficult to be blessed with a gift that is so valuable to others –

BB A gift? Is that what it is? How do you know that?

Fowles Well, everybody knows.

BB How?

Fowles Well, for one thing there are books. Your famous books on the painters of the Renaissance. Your Four Gospels, as everybody calls them.

BB Ah, you've read them then, have you?

Fowles Well, no, not yet, BB, but I promised myself that one day, when I have a little spare time –

BB A little spare time! (*Laughs.*) You'll need a great deal of spare time for my Four Gospels, 'as everybody calls them'. They are in fact my Coffins, my Four Coffins, full of dead prose and murdered – yes, murdered thoughts. (*Stops.*) But if you haven't read them, where does your knowledge of this gift from? From these conversations we have? Because I speak with such authority? But I may be speaking nonsense with authority. The gift you say I'm blessed with may be the gift of talking nonsense with authority.

Fowles Still, it's good enough for Joe.

BB And therefore good enough for you.

Fowles More than good enough for me, BB, given what I know about Joe, after all – oh, and talking of your authority – he particularly wanted me to discuss an attribution, whether you might care to reconsider –

BB Attribution?

Fowles Yes.

BB Which?

Fowles The *Adoration*, BB.

BB He wants me to re-attribute it?

Fowles Yes, from Giorgione to Titian.

BB I have attributed it to Titian.

Fowles Yes, I meant of course from Titian to –

BB No.

Fowles You won't discuss it then?

BB No. My attribution is clear and unqualified. There is nothing to discuss. If there was, I'd discuss it. I'm not a man who stands by his mistakes. Which reminds me – and proves my point – the Masaccio Joe has just sold to Mellon?

Fowles What? Oh. Yes.

BB It isn't a Masaccio.

Fowles But didn't you authenticate it?

BB Exactly. A mistake. I'm admitting it. You see?

Fowles But then – well, if Mellon finds out –

BB I shall be publishing my reasons.

Fowles Then Joe will probably have to give him his money back.

BB I expect so.

Fowles And – and you'll have to return your percentage.

BB (*after a little pause*) I regarded it as a fee.

Fowles Well, percentage or fee – it was for the authentication.

BB I will charge him nothing for altering it.

Fowles makes to say something.

That was a joke. When I have official confirmation that Mellon has returned the picture and that Joe has returned the money I shall, of course, return my commission. You see, Fowles, I can't afford to stick by my mistakes, whatever the cost. What use would I be, with a damaged reputation?

Fowles And if Joe finds someone who will support your original authentication?

BB I shan't keep quiet. I shall challenge it. And of course my word will be accepted. Because of my reputation. Explain that to Joe. And tell him if I can bear my losses, he can bear his. And I need the money and he doesn't. And tell him further – no, no, don't tell him anything further.

There is a pause.

You look unwell – are you all right?

Fowles Oh, yes, yes, thank you – I was just wondering whether there was anything else – but I'm sure there isn't – so I can leave you to the peace of I Tatti –

BB But you're staying to dinner, surely? You always stay to dinner.

Fowles Unfortunately my wife is expecting me home for tomorrow. It's her wedding anniversary, you see.

BB Hers?

Fowles Ours, I mean. We've never missed one. We've got the boys back from school especially –

BB Oh. Well then – (*Holds his hand out.*) Have a good trip back to hearth and home. And happy anniversary to Mrs Fowles. As well as yourself.

Fowles (*shaking his hand*) Thank you. And my thanks to Mrs Berenson and to Miss Mariano. Please make my farewells for me.

BB Excuse my manner this evening. If I've been a bit – anxious. (*Gestures.*) But these are anxious times, anxious times. They make me ruder than I like to be.

Fowles Oh, that's all right, I – I – well, I suppose my trouble is that I'm not Joe.

BB On the contrary, your virtue – among many virtues – is that you're not Joe.

Fowles (*laughs*) Well, thank you, BB. (*Slight pause.*) And I'll see that the outstanding sum – the eighteen thousand –

BB Eighteen and a half, I believe Miss Mariano put it at.

Fowles Eighteen and a half, yes. The moment I get back. (*Makes to say something, doesn't, goes.*)

BB stands for a moment, takes a few restless paces up and down, sits down, pours himself a glass of wine, takes a sip, grimaces as if finding it warm and sour, flips the contents of the glass onto the grass.
Mary enters during this, and stands propped on her stick, watching him.

BB (*suddenly aware of her*) Ah. You're up and about, then.

Mary Yes.

BB And – what are you doing?

Mary I was looking at you. It struck me as odd – that it was a long time since I looked at you without your seeing me.

BB Indeed? (*listening*) Fowles has gone. He's not staying for dinner. (*going to her*)

Mary Oh. Pity. I quite enjoy his company at dinner. It's all right, I can manage. (*as BB tries to take an arm*) You finished your business, then?

BB Yes, yes. He was more awkward than usual. More lift-boy.

Mary stumbles, almost falls.

BB If you let me take your arm, you wouldn't stumble.

Mary (*sweetly*) Perhaps I prefer to stumble.

BB (*barks a laugh*) Yes. Perhaps you do. But it's easier to support you than to lift you from the ground.

Mary You go in. Tell Nicky to come for me. In five minutes. (*going to seat, sitting down*) In five minutes.

BB looks towards her, hesitates, goes off. Mary sits. Lights.

SCENE TWO

BB's library. After dinner.
BB is sitting at his desk, reading the letter mentioned in Scene One. He is clearly amused.
Nicky is sitting at her desk on which there are two ledgers. She is wearing her spectacles, smoking a cigarette, making calculations, as she sorts through the pile of bills from the garden. She glances at her watch, glances at BB, goes back to her accounting.

BB (*not looking up*) Very amusing letter from Kenneth Clark. Particularly about Joe and the National Gallery. Did she have trouble getting to sleep?

Nicky Yes.

BB More than usual, you mean?

Nicky She took a little opium.

BB I wish she wouldn't.

Nicky She didn't take much. I mixed it myself. But the pain is quite bad tonight. It's been bad all day, I think.

BB Yes. We'll get the doctor over tomorrow.

Nicky She won't have him. I've already tried.

BB Then what are we to do?

Nicky She doesn't want us to do anything. Her only plan is to see her family again.

BB See the family, take to her bed, die. Is that it? (*Little pause.*) Does she know I love her?

Nicky Oh, BB, of course she does. Just as you know she loves you. And don't worry about being disagreeable. She wouldn't have you any other way.

BB Yes, yes, And so we live together in rancorous affection. Or affectionate rancour. There may be a distinction. We used to brawl, you know, when we first met –

Nicky Brawl?

BB As in bar-brawl. Fight. Physically fight.

Nicky You and Mary? Why? (*Laughs.*)

BB I don't know. It would start from almost nothing. She would find something I said particularly distasteful or wounding – it never seemed particularly distasteful or wounding to me, of course, no different from anything I'd said five minutes before, in fact said most of the time – sometimes just a laugh, or smiling, yes, my merely smiling in a certain way, maliciously I suppose, would do it – she'd be on me, slapping and kicking and scratching at me like a fishwife in a comedy. I would have to catch her wrists, virtually wrestle her to the floor, hold her down. She was very strong. Agile. A brute, in fact.

Nicky Mary – a brute! Well, what happened then – after your brawl? Did you make love?

BB Sometimes. Or we would just sit together, talking quietly about – well, della Francesca, Giotto, Rembrandt –

whatever I was working on, thinking about at the time. And life, of course. Life. Life. It's a long time since we had a conversation about life. Or Giotto. But then it's a long time since we brawled. Poor Mary.

Nicky And poor you, from your expression.

BB I sometimes wish – find myself wishing –

Nicky What?

BB Oh, I don't know – perhaps that she and I had met as unattached man and woman, and then we might never have become attached, or if we had, simply become husband and wife to each other, and left it at that.

Nicky laughs.

You find that funny?

Nicky Well, the idea that any couple could meet as man and woman, and then simply become husband and wife to each other, and leave it at that! Leave it at that! If only Adam and Eve had left it at that! (*Kisses him.*)

BB Do you still love me, then? After so many years?

Nicky Oh, stop it, BB. You know I shall always love you.

BB But you – you've never shown a hint of jealousy. I don't think I'm altogether flattered by that.

Nicky You should be flattered by the fact that I've been completely faithful.

BB I couldn't have borne it if you hadn't been.

Nicky And yet you expect me to bear your infidelities.

BB What do you mean? What infidelities? – You can't mean the Swede? The sex is really just a part of her treatment. With knobs on. (*Lets out a bark of surprised laughter.*)

Nicky looks at him.

Yes, yes, very vulgar – well, you bring it out in me. It's one of your most delightful gifts.

Nicky makes to say something, doesn't. After a pause:

What is it?

Nicky No. Perhaps this is not the evening –

BB Yes, it is the evening, it is the evening. You want to say something, so say it. Not to say it would be childish.

Nicky Very well. (*Little pause.*) Then you must listen to me, BB.

BB I listen.

Nicky When I first came here we would spend hours together, you working so intensely, I watching you, learning how to help, I was so in love with you, and I knew you knew what I was feeling, you revelled in it, I could feel you revelling in it –

BB And so? They were wonderful hours, wonderful days – you've given me wonderful years, Nicky. I know that. I tell you so. More and more often. It's a form of dotage.

Nicky And so. And so. (*Pause.*) Every time you had a female house guest – I'd know whether you'd spent the night with her by Mary's little jokes in the morning. The only times I've ever hated her was when she made those jokes – she would watch my face as I tried to find an expression for her little jokes – you at least had the grace to dodge my look. I am not complaining, I am declaring my love. The nature of it. It has been well and truly tested, from the very beginning.

BB Yes. Well then, poor Nicky, too. My poor Nicky.

Nicky (*about to go, looks at him in alarm*) I didn't mean! My darling, you look stricken! Don't look stricken – it's nothing – I wasn't complaining – just remembering – teasing –

BB No, no, it's not you, it's never you, Nicky, my darling, it's just that I feel as if – as if – I am losing, losing a sense of myself, can it be? That there is nothing there, that really I have done nothing in my life, my life, except acquire, acquire my collections, acquire my reputation, acquire my I Tatti. Just a few hours ago, there I was, with little Fowles, negotiating about money and reputation and the painting we stole from the church and strutting my honour at him over Mellon's Masaccio but I could see that for him there was really nothing to choose between Joe and me, except that Joe is rich, and that I, suddenly, am becoming poor. There is a voice I hear, a piping voice, no, a shrill, jeering voice, that says well, well, it doesn't matter, nothing matters, you and Joe, Joe and you, you have earned nothing, you deserve nothing but each other –

Nicky This – this is all because you're having to worry about money, and it's wrong, you should never, ever, have to worry about money, it's an appalling indignity. You have earned and deserved everything you want, and you should have it – how can you speak of yourself and Joe, Joe and yourself? Joe is a businessman, a salesman, an entrepreneur, he is only important in that he is useful to you, and you have every right to use him, every right, because you, my darling BB, are a great man. You've taught people how to look at a painting and see into the soul of artists long dead –

BB No, no. Please no!

Nicky Well, you have. Yes, you have.

BB My darling Nicky, you are a Catholic and half-Russian, you believe that you and I and even Joe have souls, but I, for one, do not. I have only eyes – (*pointing to them*) – that can see. A brain – (*tapping it*) – that can think. A memory – (*wagging his hand over his face*) – that can connect. I have no soul. It is not only the word that has come to disgust me. It is the very thought of the thing itself. It distracts attention from man's achievement, which is that he has evolved from the slime without benefit of soul. He has only his natural faculties, and his determination to cultivate them. No soul. No God. Just this, this, and that. (*pointing to his eyes, his heart and face*) And now – now – (*gestures helplessly*) – they offer me nothing that can help me. Or so it would seem. So perhaps I could use a soul, after all, eh?

Nicky I've seen you a thousand times looking at a painting. Your face – your face has been full of soul, my darling. As a child – in Lithuania – when you used to wander about in the woods – what you described, the way you've described it –

BB I described a child in the woods, suddenly seeing the light. I saw the light. With my eyes. Just as now, if I were to look out of the window, I would see darkness. And one day soon we will see the darkness in the light. One morning or afternoon, in the sunshine, there will be the duck quacking at our gates. And then, however bright the sun, we will be living in an eclipse, a man-made eclipse, another human achievement to wonder at. Again without benefit of soul. Quack, quack. (*Lifts a finger, listens attentively.*) Is that a motor? In the drive?

Nicky (*suddenly realising, looks surreptitiously at her watch*) I can't hear anything. (*Goes to window.*) I can't see anything. No. No car.

BB One is always expecting the police. Those are the times we live in. (*Listens again.*) Are you sure?

Nicky Yes. But I'll go and look, if you want – it's time I checked on Mary. (*Hurries out.*)

BB listens again, makes to go to the window, then forces himself back to his desk, hears something again, goes to the window, peers out at an awkward angle, obviously sees nothing, then goes to the door, opens it, listens. Clearly does hear something. Braces himself angrily, makes to go out, checks himself, closes the door quietly, thinks, goes to his desk, picks up the letter.

Duveen (*offstage*) Miss Mariano, good evening.

There is a knock on the door. BB pays no attention.
There is another knock, slightly louder. BB pays no attention.
Duveen enters. He is magnificently dressed, or appears to be, from what is visible of his clothes under his astrakhan coat – bottom of trousers, shoes, etc. He is wearing a silk scarf, a flower in his buttonhole, top hat in hand, and a walking stick. He is carrying a shiny, large, oblong case in black leather, with a handle, a form of briefcase.

BB (*goes on studying letter*) Just a minute, if you please.

Duveen (*puts down case, stands waiting*)

BB turns, looks at him. There is a pause. Duveen holds out his arms.

Come, BB! BB, come. Let us embrace!

BB Don't be ridiculous. And how did you get in? Through a window?

Duveen I was about to ring the bell when your enchanting Miss Mariano heard me on the doorstep. She has such a smile – how I envy you, BB, to have such a smile in the house

BB Nevertheless, she knows you're not welcome at I Tatti. She should have turned you away. I shall be very angry with her.

Duveen No, you mustn't be. Mary called out and she had to run to her. Fowles tells me that Mary is not well. I'm sorry to hear it.

BB She has a problem with her digestion, nothing for you to bother yourself with. But you're incomplete. Something's missing. Oh, of course, your cigar. Where is your cigar?

Duveen Ah, the doctors – the doctors forbid! Though I keep one about me – (*Takes one out of his pocket.*) – for comfort. The occasional – (*Sniffs it, puts it back in his pocket.*) You are not surprised to see me, then?

BB I happened to be thinking about you. You arrived. On the dot.

Duveen On the dot?

BB On the dot of the thought.

Duveen And what was the thought?

BB It was occasioned by this. (*Holds up letter.*)

Duveen What is it?

BB A letter from Kenneth.

Duveen Kenneth?

BB He keeps me in touch.

Duveen Really? What does he say?

BB He says here that he thinks you are about to lose your trusteeship.

Duveen What? What do you mean?

BB Your trusteeship of the National Gallery. Kenneth thinks you're about to lose it.

Duveen It is gossip and rumour. Nothing has been settled. It'll become evident, when they look into it properly, that my relationship with the Gallery is completely *comme il faut*, completely proper and *comme il faut*, however certain – (*Gestures.*) – ill-wishers may wish to make it appear otherwise.

BB Ah well, in England, you know, the *appearance* of impropriety is the impropriety. You would have understood that if you hadn't spent so much time in America. In America you've got into the habit of thinking of yourself as a sort of king, a position only possible nowadays in a capitalist democracy. And then when you come to England and play the buffoon –

Duveen I behave as I believe. That all men are born equal.

BB That is what I mean by buffoon. And they love you for it, or so you like to boast – your enthusiasm, your vulgarity, your patter of money and art and – there is the matter of the Sassetta panels.

Duveen The Sassetta panels, what about them?

BB Kenneth says in your role of trustee you have been negotiating their purchase for the Gallery.

Duveen Yes? Well? I am proud of doing so. They will be a splendid acquisition.

BB But it has come out they are in fact owned by you and it is therefore from yourself that you are buying them for the Gallery. He writes that this has made your position untenable. He is quite upset, because personally he is very fond of you.

Duveen But this is nonsense, nonsense! If I chose to sell the panels on the commercial market, I would make a far greater profit. In fact I will lose money by selling them to the National Gallery. Yes, probably lose money. And certainly time and energy, which I should be hoarding. At my time of life hoarding my time, my money! I have done nothing wrong! In fact I am making sacrifices for the Gallery. It is a sacred trust, to be a trustee –

BB Exactly, a sacred trust, a sacred trust, and yet here you are, talking of your time and your money, your profit and your loss, like a mere tradesman. They have been letting you enter and leave by the wrong door, Joe. In future you'll have to go around to the back.

Duveen Is that what Kenneth says?

BB His language is less delicate.

Duveen (*laughs*) Yes, yes, he has a sharp pen. Well – I'll see him as soon as I get back, I shall sort it out. I shall dispose of the panels somewhere else. By the time they get into the Gallery my name will no longer be attached to them.

BB I doubt that your name will still be attached to the trusteeship.

Duveen They need me.

BB They needed you.

Duveen I'll tell you what is odd, BB – that of the two of us, the scholar and the tradesman, it is you that should be the cynic.

BB It saves one a great deal of disappointment. (*Sees the case. Gesturing*) What is that?

Duveen That? Oh – something I was hoping you'd enjoy casting your eye over later.

BB Perhaps now would be best. I shall be going to bed shortly.

Duveen Very well, you shall have your way, as you always do – (*going to case, stops*) – but first let me finish a little business. I have brought a cheque for the sum that you and Fowles established as outstanding. In fact, I went through the figures again with Fowles, you and Fowles were out by a thousand. In your favour, BB, I am sorry to say. Where is it? (*searching through his pockets*) It is certainly here – never mind, I'll find it before I go. By which time I hope that we will be partners.

BB stares at him.

That is why I am here. I've come by train, boat and car to offer you a partnership, BB.

BB A partnership?

Duveen A full partnership.

BB That would mean, in my understanding, that would mean that I would receive a percentage on any transaction you completed, whether I participated in it or not?

Duveen Yes. That is what it means. That is the full meaning of full partnership.

BB And what would be the percentage of this full partnership?

Duveen Sixteen per cent . . . eighteen per cent . . . twenty, then.

BB But I assume that my commissions on any transactions that came your way through my – influence – would remain as they are.

Duveen Well, of course.

BB And if I ceased to interest myself in any such transactions –

Duveen You would have to waive your commission.

BB Naturally. I could scarcely claim a commission on transactions I hadn't undertaken.

Duveen Any more than you could undertake transactions without claiming a commission.

BB By which you mean?

Duveen No independent transactions. No deals with other dealers. In other words.

BB And if there were no deals at all?

Duveen shrugs.

BB But I would retain my partnership?

Duveen Such is your value, BB. And if you decide to involve yourself directly in any deal, your commission would be increased. As befits a full partner.

BB By how much?

Duveen It would be doubled. It would become fifteen per cent.

BB Doubled would be twenty per cent.

Duveen Doubled, I mean, from when we first entered into our arrangement.

BB I would prefer it to be from when we last nearly terminated it.

Duveen You see.

BB See what?

Duveen How helpless you always make me feel. There should be such a simple opposition, the trader and man of the world against the scholar and recluse – you should have no chance with me at all, and yet I end up yielding everything, everything.

BB The value of my name has depended on its not being publicly connected to yours. Our partnership must not be allowed to affect that.

Duveen You mean you wish our partnership to be confidential?

BB Of course.

Duveen So that your authentications will retain their integrity?

BB Of course.

Duveen But you will continue to authenticate?

BB Of course.

Duveen Well, that all seems clear and above board.

BB And it will be. I have no intention of letting our partnership compromise my authentications. They will be authentic.

Duveen As your retractions are authentic. Fowles tells me I will have to reimburse Mellon for his Masaccio. To the tune of half a million, perhaps.

BB Your consolation is that it is not a Masaccio. And your honour is preserved.

Duveen Our honour now. Our honour, BB.

BB Our honour. Which is confidential to us. Our private honour, therefore.

Duveen So. You accept then?

BB I accept.

Duveen stands up, opens his arms.

May we do it my way, Joe?

Offers his hand. Duveen takes it. They shake. Duveen pulls BB to him, embraces him.

Lights.

Curtain.

Act Two

The same. A second later, BB is still enfolded in Duveen's embrace. BB detaches himself.

Duveen Well then. That concludes – that seems to conclude with everything settled between us. Settled at last. (*Stares at BB. Moved.*)

BB Apart that is, from the cheque. Eighteen and a half thousand pounds – (*Makes a little gesture, with his finger.*)

Duveen Nineteen and a half thousand pounds. (*Pats his pocket.*)

BB looks at him, puzzled, then, as if remembering, feels in his pocket, takes out cheque.

You see what comes when you cuddle your partner? Hah!

BB (*laughs*) Well, I suppose this calls for a drink. (*Moves towards drinks.*)

Duveen Not for me, no drink – no cigar – perhaps a drop of water, though. Eh? No, no, you're right, one must do something, yes, one can at least hold and smell – (*Takes out cigar, sniffs it, rolls it about.*) – and a drop of grappa to go with it, just a drop – that local grappa if you still serve it in I Tatti.

BB It hasn't been touched since you were last here – (*Brings Duveen glass of grappa.*)

Duveen (*sniffing it, then sniffing cigar*) Ah! Ah! Those were the days, those were the days. But still, this is the life!

BB, coming back with drink, sees case.

BB Now what is that?

Duveen In a minute, in a minute, now let us just be, just be . . . So good – so good to be here again, talking together again in a way that we used to.

BB Yes, well – much of the time we didn't talk, Joe. We often ended up shouting into each other's faces. Once or twice I found myself on the verge of hitting you.

Duveen You mustn't blame only yourself, BB. There were flashes of intemperance on my part, too. It's really because we're so fond of each other. For thirty years we've been this and that, on and off, sometimes a good marriage, sometimes a bad one – but how could we not be matched for life! When you think of what you do, and then of what I do.

BB And how is Elsie?

Duveen All the better for your asking, thank you, BB. She will rejoice at our news. I used to be quite jealous – she admires you so much. But though I could never do what you do – I haven't the eye, the mind, the memory – the genius, yes? But then what is genius but unique? But then what I do – what I do – well, not many men can do as I do, eh BB, give me that – not unique, but the best. But – to tell you the truth, I sometimes wonder if I can do it any more – the collectors now, the sort of men who want to acquire great works – Frick and Huntingdon were difficult men, difficult, but at least I could teach them, yes, that was my gift, that made me the best – I could teach men like Frick and Huntingdon the value of what they were buying – I persuaded them that they – well, that they had – (*Meets BB's eye.*)

BB Souls.

Duveen Yes. Yes, I know what you think of the word, but Frick and Mellon had something, whatever you call it, that a man like Kress hasn't even a whiff of. Not a whiff of a whatever you call it in Kress. That is my point.

BB Kress? Who is Kress?

Duveen Kress is the new man. The new American. He is the future. He is Mr Five-and-Dime. Kress.

BB Oh. Those stores.

Duveen All across America. In every state. And here's something. Let me tell you something. When he was in – he was in . . . (*Looks at cigar, puzzled, fumbles in his pocket, stops, stares at BB, bewildered.*)

BB Joe?

Duveen What?

BB We seem to have lost you.

Duveen Lost me? What do you mean? What was I talking about? You've distracted me.

BB It was your cigar that distracted you. I believe you were looking for your matches.

Duveen They are here. I have them. (*showing him matches*)

BB Then perhaps you should use one.

Duveen Oh no, BB, no, no, don't tempt me. The doctors forbid. (*Puts matches and cigar back in his pocket. As he does he mumbles something, and the word 'devil' is just audible.*)

BB What? What are you saying?

Duveen Mmm?

BB About the devil. You said something about the devil, I didn't quite hear it.

Duveen The devil, eh, the devil, did I, well, I probably said let him take the hindmost, eh, BB? (*Roars out an odd laugh, stops, starting into sudden fluency.*) Yes, there he is sitting in a café in Algiers –

BB Who?

Duveen Kress, Kress, Samuel Kress – I was just talking about him, when you – (*Gestures irritably.*) And along comes one of those street traders, selling shawls – (*Imitates.*) – shawls, shawls, beautiful shawls – pushing them along in his handcart. So our man Kress, he can't let the opportunity slip by, even in a café in Algiers on his holiday. With a trader who trades he has to trade a little, what else is there for him to do? So he begins, how much are they? Ah, and in dollars how much, ah, and if he buys two shawls now how much in discount, and the discount for three how much, how much, say, if he buys half the stock he sees before him, would he get a couple from the half he leaves behind thrown in free, ah, and how many shawls does this trader have apart from what's on his hand-barrow. Ah, well then, put that stock on top of this stock, how much discount? So on it goes and on, until at the end, he makes his purchase of seven thousand, three hundred and fifty shawls of which two hundred and fifty are completely free, another two thousand, one hundred and fifty shawls discounted down to almost their true worth, the deal of a lifetime, because when he's sold every single one of them, which he will do, he'll have made a clear profit of three hundred and forty eight dollars, which will be a seventy per cent profit. That's it, you see, that's the point, for this man of many millions, he will have pulled off a remarkable coup of a seventy per cent profit. Who cares whether it's in millions or in cents, that's what matters to him, that's the spirit of him, that's the – the whatever of him.

BB But surely, Joe, you will educate him. You will make him worthy of his purchases, yes?

Duveen I am trying. I am trying. I am trying. But listen to this, BB. Six months ago I let him into my private gallery, into the very heart of it, where I keep one of my most sacred shrines. My Amico di Sandro. (*Nods at BB.*) So you had designated it, BB. I folded my hands, so. (*Folds them.*) And gestured thus. (*Gestures prayerfully with his hands.*) And he looked at this – this truly – of a grace, a charm, a religious tenderness, of a holiness and a lustrousness – as I said to him – whispered to him. Holiness. Lustrousness. (*whispering intently*) Luminousness. And he squinted at it for eight, nine, ten seconds, and he said, 'How much?' So. So I doubled the sum that came into my head and added fifty thousand. He said, the room back there, the one we came through, there were six paintings in the room, who were they by? Well, I said, there were two Titians, a Gainsborough, a Tintoretto, a Botticelli and an Uccello. And how much are those, he asked? Well, I said, and I began to give him the price of each. Ah, he said, but if I bought the lot? I named a price, a price, a sum, a sum so huge – ah, he said, now if I bought this sacred and luminous masterpiece here, and three of those other masterpieces in there, what kind of discount would you give me? Ah, and now if I took five and the sacred and luminous masterpiece, ah, and if I took all six and the sacred and luminous, what would you throw in free, and what discount on the other six. And so – and so – I was the street trader in Algiers, BB, I began to bargain, yes, before I knew it, I was bargaining with Mr Five-and-Dime over Amico di Sandro and a fistful of price-reduced masterpieces – no, no, I shouted, no, no, this is not for sale, those are not for sale, not to you, no, they're already sold, they're going to Mellon, all of them, to Mellon. Oh, Mr Mellon, he said, well, why didn't you just say so in the first place? Because I've only just realised, I said, and I haven't told him yet. Well, how do you know he'll buy them, he said? Because, I said, because I'll tell him that if he doesn't they'll go to you. Ah, he said. Ah. He didn't say another word except goodbye and thank you. On the pavement. Well, of course, since then I've had to allow him some droppings from my table, a tidbit here, a tidbit there, just to keep him quiet, but you know the story about the appetite, and what it feeds on. And with Frick dead, Mellon dying, what can I do but trade with Mr Five-and-Dime?

BB Mellon is dying?

Duveen But not dead. Not yet dead, thank God! We can't have him dead until he's finished his life's work, on which his immortality depends. A few paintings for him still to acquire. One in particular. Yes, one will be enough, if it is the right one. And then he may go. In peace and triumph. With one of the world's greatest collections as his memorial.

BB One will be enough?

Duveen If it is the right one.

BB (*glancing towards the case*) And have you brought it with you, by any chance?

Duveen I have.

BB That is the pleasure you promised me.

Duveen To cap your evening. You will not be disappointed. (*Gets up, goes to the case, looks around, sees a stand, on which there is a picture underneath a light that is off.*) May I? (*Turns on light, looks at picture as he removes it from stand.*) Goya. But you detest Goya.

BB That's why I keep him in the dark. I'm thinking of writing a short paper. (*indicating a corner*)

Duveen places Goya where BB indicated, adjusts the stand for best visibility, goes to his case, takes a bunch of keys out of his pocket, uses a succession of keys to open case, each clicking, opens lid ceremonially, takes picture out. Carries it to the stand, arranges it there, steps away, looks towards BB, who hasn't moved.

Duveen Don't you want to see what it is?

BB I know what it is. Your lift-boy let the cat out of the bag.

Duveen Well, what?

BB It is a copy of *The Adoration of the Shepherds*. By Titian.

Duveen No, it is not.

BB Well, what then? (*Comes over, looks, looks more closely, in disbelief.*)

Duveen You see, BB – not a copy!

BB You've been carrying this in your luggage – in cars, boats – through customs –

Duveen It was thrilling. Took me back to the old days, BB, when Mary had the false bottoms to her suitcases, and her hat-boxes for the icons.

BB And you smuggled it all the way here just to give me pleasure?

Duveen And does it give you pleasure?

BB Yes. But is it the only reason?

Duveen Well, you already know from Fowles, then – I wanted the pleasure of your opinion of it, after you've given it a fresh look.

BB Ah! Then I will give it a fresh look.

Duveen waits, impatient.
BB goes to painting, studies it with great concentration. He straightens, looks at Duveen.

Duveen Well. What?

BB Well what, what?

Duveen What did you see? What struck you? Something struck you! I saw it strike you!

BB Yes. The exceptional genius of the pupil that is escaping the genius of the master. This is an act of escape, yes. Everywhere the influence of the master, and yet – and yet – it is a creation that is completely the pupil's. A hatching, a moment of sublime hatching. That is what I suddenly felt. As I'd never felt it before. All the times I'd looked at it. However hard I looked. Never had that moment. Thank you, Joe. It was the last thing I expected this evening. Especially when you have already given me so much.

Duveen says nothing.

I am glad it is going to Mellon. It will be a great addition to his collection. And congratulations to you, too, Joe, are of course in order.

Duveen (*coldly*) And to yourself, too, as partner. Twenty per cent of the commission will be yours.

BB Generous of you, Joe, but I must decline. This is something you achieved before we reached our agreement.

Duveen Not that you will be losing much, eh?

BB However much or little, it is entirely yours. (*Little pause.*) Well, perhaps I could take my old percentage, if you see fit to use my name. If you think Mellon wants my name attached –

Duveen You are laughing at me! Do you think I have come all the way here to be laughed at! (*shouting*)

BB What about? What am I laughing at you about, Joe, please?

Duveen (*pulls himself together*) All right then. Let us discuss it calmly.

BB I am calm.

Duveen You realise now that you are quite alone.

BB Quite alone? Really? In what respect?

Duveen *The Adoration of the Shepherds* has been authenticated as a Giorgione by every other expert in the field. But most particularly by Richard Offner. Not even you can deny his authority.

BB Indeed not! Nor his integrity. I'm always sorry when he and I disagree. But there we are. I for Titian, he for Giorgione. An interesting debate. History, I suppose, will decide between us.

Duveen I can't wait for history. I need it settled now. Once and for all. No loose ends.

BB Why?

Duveen You know why. Mellon wants a Giorgione, not a Titian. The difference between a Giorgione and a

Titian is a difference of – of – hundreds of thousands. More. A million.

BB Why?

Duveen Why? What the devil do you mean, why? You know perfectly well why! Because there are lots of Titians and very few, very few – (*Gestures to painting.*)

BB But surely what matters is that this is a glory in itself, whether painted by the prolific Titian, or Giorgione – who, I've often thought, would always have hoarded his genius, only releasing it after long intervals of creative contemplation, and that there would be very little of him, even if he hadn't died young.

Duveen That's as may be, that's as may be – the fact is he did die young, and – and we owe it to him, to our understanding of his genius, to give him the reputation he deserves.

BB But of course.

Duveen By assigning to his name his few and precious works.

BB But because they're so few and precious we must be particularly careful not to be careless – or greedy – in our assignations. Grant one here – (*gesturing to painting*) – merely to increase its market worth, and soon we'll be granting another one, and then another one – why, even in your own terms, Joe, that finally becomes bad business.

Duveen There isn't another one, there is only this one, and Mellon wants it as a Giorgione, which it is, it is – it is a Giorgione, not a Titian, and Mellon should be allowed to have it as a Giorgione – he doesn't want it as a Titian. (*Little pause.*) At least accept the possibility that you might be wrong.

BB I always accept that possibility. Good God, Joe, these are matters of opinion. Informed opinion. I acknowledge a mistake when there is further information that alters my opinion. Which was the case with the Masaccio. There has been no further information to alter my opinion that *The Adoration of the Shepherds* was painted by Titian. And I have to back my own opinions, Joe, don't I? Or what would be the use of me? What would have been the use of me to you, in the past? The profitable past? I have been, you might say, your golden opinion.

Duveen You admit you've made mistakes. What's more, BB, what's more, I've known times when you've gone where the advantage is. (*Little pause.*) The profit. (*Little pause.*) Sometimes when there's been only the slightest, the very slightest, doubt.

BB I hope that that is not true.

Duveen I could specify them. (*Little pause.*) I will specify them. For instance the Bellini –

BB I said it was conceivable that it was not a Bellini.

Duveen Then say the same of this. Say it is conceivable – it is conceivable – that it is a Giorgione. I'll settle for that.

BB You mean Mellon will settle for that?

Duveen He would. I'd see to it.

BB Really? And he – you – wouldn't expect me to withdraw my previous attribution to Titian?

Duveen (*after a long pause*) No. That won't be necessary.

BB Really?

Duveen You need do nothing.

BB Ah. (*Little pause.*) I see. You will announce that it is a Giorgione, you will announce the source – the eminent source – Offner.

Duveen Sources. Sources. Offner and everyone but you. Everyone that matters but you.

BB And as long as I hold my tongue –

Duveen Hold your tongue, BB? As soon ask a river to hold its flow.

BB Well then – we've come a long way. From begging for my authentication of Giorgione to allowing me freedom to repeat my view that it is a Titian. Can that be right, Joe? Do I understand you?

Duveen Privately. Privately you can confirm it as a Titian. (*Goes to painting, almost cuddling it.*) Even though you are not a Titian. You are a Giorgione. On every centimetre it is evident, to my eye, Giorgione himself is crying out, this is by me, this is me, here I am, at my greatest, why deny me, how can you deny me my being who I am? But you (*to BB*) are at liberty to deny me my being who I am. Privately you can pass me off as Titian. You have my permission. You have my blessing.

BB Thank you.

Duveen Just as long as you publish nothing. That is all I ask.

BB nods.

You agree, then?

BB (*glances at the painting, then as if drawn to it against his will, goes to it, studies it*) You realise that I've already admitted that without Giorgione this painting could not exist.

Duveen Ah – well, if you would say that! Then – then I'd say that you have already earned your partnership, BB!

BB Earned it?

Duveen Honoured. Honoured would be the better word.

BB Would it? (*Turns back to painting.*) These faces – the faces of the two kneeling shepherds – however hard I try, I never remember them properly. I retain an impression of intensity, of devotion, but I never have a sense of them in their individuality, their eyes, their features, their expressions – and now of course I realise why. Because of course he doesn't show us their faces. See, Joe. No faces.

Duveen (*peers*) No. No faces. Is that good or bad?

BB It is magnificent. You see how everything – (*Stops.*) So this is our understanding. We know, you and I, Joe, that I believe this to be a Titian, but on the other hand, in order to honour and earn, earn and honour our new partnership why not, why not, for God's sake, nod it through as a Giorgione. No need to publish or even speak the lie, just a nod that nods it through, a nod in my sleep, even Homer nodded once or twice, now and then, why shouldn't BB nod, just once, now – what difference? Think of Europe now, think of what awaits us tomorrow, what difference then a little nod in a Tuscan library at midnight, a little nod from BB to Joe?

Duveen No difference.

BB Except to you and me.

Duveen Except to you and me. (*Pause.*) You don't even have to nod. You don't even have to look the other way. You can say what you like to whomever you like, as long as you don't say it in print. What could be better? What could be easier?

BB And I will have earned and honoured my partnership.

Duveen Yes.

BB shakes his head.

What are you doing?

BB I am shaking my head.

Duveen Why?

BB Because it is the opposite of a nod.

Duveen But why?

BB Because you have been trading, Joe. Since you came here you have been trading the partnership for a nod.

Duveen You mean, it's a matter simply of my having put it into words? (*Laughs.*) You can't mean that?

BB says nothing.

I never spoke them.

BB You spoke them.

Duveen I didn't mean them. You misunderstood.

BB You meant them. I understood.

Duveen And therefore you'll – what will you do?

BB I shall publish to the world my view that *The Adoration of the Shepherds* is a masterpiece of Titian's apprenticeship to his great master, Giorgione.

Duveen It will go to Kress. To Kress. It will go to Kress. He will buy it and exhibit it – God knows where he will exhibit it – (*Laughs.*) but wherever it will be, it will be an insult. Furthermore, he will probably exhibit it as a Giorgione.

BB Then you have the ideal purchaser. One who doesn't give a fig for my views. Still, I can see that it's not a negotiation that you care to be associated with, even by default. Certainly not at this stage of your career, eh, Joe, with your trusteeship of the National Gallery and your reputation already – (*gestures sympathetically*)

Duveen You think doing this will save yours, is that it? Well then, it's time somebody told you, BB, you no longer have a reputation. Except with Mellon, alas, a dying man clinging to his sad old habits. But among the tellers of reputations, yours is pretty well known these days for the uses to which it has been put over the years. It's losing its value in the marketplace, even. You will have to skulk here in I Tatti with diminishing funds and when you die your collection will be dispersed around the world and I Tatti will become what, an old people's home, a hotel for American or German tourists. Perhaps there will be a suite or a public room named after you, yes, the Bernard Berenson Lounge, where businessmen can do deals and then take cocktails with their weekend girlfriends. And as for your gardens, the chapel – (*Makes gesture.*)

BB I like the thought of the weekend girlfriends. That will be preserving something of my spirit. (*Little pause.*)

Duveen Or perhaps you hope your reputation will live on through your writings, your Four Gospels. Your own masterpieces. But there are certain doubts there, are there not? About attribution? Rumours have been circulating for some time that the hand that held the pen was not always yours.

BB The moment I hear that *The Adoration of the Shepherds* has been ascribed to Giorgione, I shall fire off a contradiction. In fact I shall probably write the contradiction as soon as you leave. Along with a copy for Mellon. Finished business, merely requiring posting.

Duveen goes to the painting to take it. BB lets out an involuntary cry.

Duveen What?

BB Leave it a little longer.

Duveen Why?

BB So that I can look at it a little longer.

Duveen Why?

BB Just a few minutes, Joe.

Duveen I would prefer to be on my way.

BB Joe, Joe, you're being petty. That is not you.

Duveen hesitates, replaces the picture.

BB Thank you. (*Turns away.*)

Duveen And what did you see this time?

BB Only the picture. No names, no dates, no history. Only the picture. Now I have it here – (*touching head*) – as it should be. Worthless. Beyond worth. Mine, for whenever I need it.

Duveen I've always longed to look into you as you look into paintings. But your eyes are never still. Can't you keep them still?

BB (*coming over to him*) I think I can keep them still when I look into yours.

They stare into each other's eyes, BB smiling, Duveen frowning with concentration. BB breaks away.

Duveen I haven't finished!

BB I saw what you wanted me to see. How long do you have?

Duveen (*goes to chair, sits down, as if suddenly collapsed. His speech becomes feebler*) Five years ago they said I would last three months. The five years are now up, I believe.

BB I am sorry.

Duveen Thank you.

BB But I can't buy you a further period of life by changing my opinion about the attribution of a painting, can I?

Duveen And if you could, would you?

BB For your life?

Duveen Any life?

BB For the life of someone I loved, almost certainly.

Duveen But certainly not for mine?

BB (*laughs*) Oh Joe, really, you're being disgusting. You'll probably have yellow eyes for another five years. Ten.

Duveen I shall be dead within three months. You have my word on it.

BB Very well. I accept it, as always, your word.

Duveen Thank you. Is it possible perhaps to say goodbye to Mary? I can't imagine another opportunity, and I've always had the greatest affection . . . It would mean a lot to me, BB.

BB I'd rather you didn't. It would mean waking her and – she's easily agitated, these days.

Duveen A kiss, perhaps, on her sleeping forehead? I'll be very quiet, very careful.

BB (*hesitates*) Her sleep is too precious. I can't risk it. I'm sorry, Joe. I'll say your goodbye for you, in the morning.

Duveen And will you tell her what you've thrown away? Fowles tells me that she's concerned about her children. And her grandchildren. She needs money for them. I know she always looks to me when money is needed. Well, I shall have to write to her and explain that it is not my fault that I cannot help her. (*Goes to the painting, takes it to the case, begins to put it in.*)

BB Write, by all means. She can sometimes read her letters. Mostly I read them out to her.

Duveen It is that serious, then?

BB As serious as your own condition, I would think.

Mary enters. She is in a dressing gown, her hair loose.

Mary I knew someone had come, Nicky said I'd dreamed it – (*going to him*) – but I didn't dream it was you, dear Joe!

Duveen Yes, here I am – (*as he embraces her*) – in the flesh!

Mary And just what's needed, just to feel you – (*touching his cheeks*) – in I Tatti again. We don't know where we are any more, with those two dreadful men and their hateful politics and Jew-baiting and threats of war – we can't really be in our Italy, our beloved Italy, can we? We're in some nightmare other country – what are we to do, Joe, what's to become of us?

Duveen I don't know, my dear, these are terrible times, terrible – but then – but then as my old uncle in Delft used to say, whatever we do the world goes on spinning, each day has its tomorrows, and each tomorrow will have its yesterdays, whether we're on the earth or under it.

Mary (*laughs*) Well, thank your Delft uncle, perhaps it sounds more consoling in Dutch.

Duveen No, it sounds more depressing in Dutch, but he said it in Yiddish, if he said it at all – I have only my mother's word for it.

Mary Oh, yes, yes, I say much the same to my little Roger. But has he offered you anything, a glass of wine –

BB My dear, you shouldn't be up, you were feeling a little sickly.

Mary You are staying the night, aren't you? BB, tell Nicky to get Joe's old room ready –

BB He can't. He's just leaving.

Mary Oh Joe!

BB A car awaits him, the train, the boat –

Mary Well then, what are you doing here like this, just popping in without warning –

Duveen I had a little plan that I thought might interest BB. But alas, my dear –

BB He wanted my opinion on a painting. That's all.

Mary Really? Which?

BB One on which I'd already given my opinion, as it turns out, so really the matter is closed, Joe was just taking his leave and you should be in bed. Does Nicky know you're running about like this?

Mary (*to Joe*) Which painting?

Duveen gestures to case. Mary goes over to look down.

Oh. Oh yes. Of course. It had to be, hadn't it? (*gazing at picture*) Oh! Oh! How I love her face. How did he do it? Oh, I wish we could keep it! – Well – (*Puts it reverently back in the box.*) – at least I'll be able to claim that once, for a few minutes, we had Giorgione here in I Tatti.

Duveen Hah!

BB It is a Titian. In my view. Which is the view that matters. As far as Joe is concerned. (*Goes over to case, puts painting in, closes it, brings it to Duveen.*)

Duveen Though I should mention, may I mention BB, to Mary that I came first and foremost to offer you a partnership. A full partnership.

BB Perhaps you should also mention that the offer was withdrawn.

Mary Why?

BB Because I refused to change my opinion.

Mary But surely, Joe, you know BB well enough to know that he could never, ever –

Duveen Of course I do, my dear. Of course I know my BB, I don't ask him to change his opinion, I merely ask him to refrain from publishing it again. He has published it once, surely that is enough?

Mary Ah. But you want him to keep quiet now other people are saying it's a Giorgione –

Duveen Not quiet, my dear, he can tell anyone and everyone, *tout le monde*, as long as he doesn't announce it in an unsolicited formal statement signed by himself. That is all I ask. That is all!

Mary I don't understand these tumults between you, I don't, when really you're so fond of each other, you have such good times together, jolly times, and yet you always, always have to go through silly little squabbles before you work things out, which you always do. Come, listen to each other, talk to each other, be kind to me. (*to Joe mainly*)

Duveen My dear, who could resist – the offer is renewed, here, in front of you, Mary, my dear. Of a full partnership. In the house of Duveen.

They look towards BB.

BB Tomorrow morning I send to all the relevant publications, and to Mellon himself, a brief letter stating that in my opinion the Giorgione is not a Titian but a Giorgione – (*realising*) – that the Titian is not a Giorgione but a Titian, rather.

Duveen (*lowers his head*) And so, Mary my dear – (*taking her hand*) – what can I say? I know how hard it's going to be for you and yours, but I think I have to leave this matter now, concluded to everyone's dissatisfaction –

Mary (*clutching hand, in a low, urgent voice*) Joe, dear Joe, give him a chance to think, just a few days, please, please!

BB (*turning back*) May I remind you, Mary, that in this house, here, in I Tatti, we try to make beggars welcome, but we never beg for ourselves, particularly from beggars, especially from rich beggars, and most especially from rich and dishonourable beggars!

There is a silence.

Duveen Oh, that reminds me – In case I don't see her again – (*Takes box from his pocket.*) – a little something for your charming Miss Mariano – in recognition of her many years of kindness to me, so unexpected in one so young. (*Gestures.*)

Mary So young? She's forty-three.

Duveen Forty-three is she, indeed? Then so much younger than ourselves, I must admit. It's nothing, really – from an auction in Boston, a widow's estate, my eye was caught by its oddity and charm, the way it seemed to smile up at me – and so I couldn't help thinking of Miss Mariano –

Mary May I see it? (*Comes over, holds out her hand.*)

Duveen places it in her hand.

Mary (*studying it in a professional manner*) But it's French, Louis Quinze, worth a good two, two and a half – and this is for Nicky? Boston, did you say, but it's certainly French –

Nicky (*enters*) Oh Mary, here you are! What are you doing, you promised me you wouldn't get up –

Mary Joe's got something for you, here – Put it on, Nicky, let's see what it looks like when it's on you – (*Makes to hand it to her.*) No, Joe, you must do it, as it's your – (*Gestures.*) You put it on her.

Duveen May I?

Nicky (*makes small gesture to resist, attempts a smile*) Of course.

Duveen Now where do you think – well, of course I suppose this is the usual – (*Fumbles with it clumsily.*)

Mary Like pinning a medal on a soldier. (*Sketches a salute.*)

Duveen No, my fingers are thumbs, you'd better do it yourself, my dear. (*Gives brooch to Nicky.*)

Nicky puts the brooch on deftly.

Mary Now let us look. My dear – your hand – it's covering –

Nicky lowers her hand.

Duveen (*clamping his cigar in his mouth*) Gorgeous, gorgeous, quite gorgeous, don't you think, BB? Eh, BB? What do you say?

BB turns away.

Mary (*standing by Duveen*) No, just a minute – don't move, my dear – be still! (*sharply. Considers Nicky.*) Not quite right.

Duveen Really? You think so? What's the matter?

Mary Rather common, I think, now I see it on.

Duveen Well, of course Miss Mariano has so much natural – natural physical –

Mary I may be wrong. What do you think, Nicky, my dear, as you're the one who has to wear it?

Nicky Well, I can't see it, can I, but – (*breaking, plucking it off*) – it feels, it feels somewhat inappropriate, I'm sorry, thank you. Thank you.

BB lets out a snort.

Mary (*taking it from Nicky's hand, as she holds it out to Joe*) I'll have it! Well, if Joe wants to give it away, and Nicky doesn't want it –

BB Not too common, after all, then.

Mary Not for the older woman, my dear – we need a touch of oddity and charm on our bosoms, smiling up at you young men. Unless Joe minds, of course, do you, Joe?

Duveen I'm delighted, my dear, that it's found a home on one of the ladies of the household.

Mary (*comes to him, embraces him*) I have to hug you tightly, tightly, dear Joe, dear Joe, because this may be the last time, the very last time – (*Step away.*) Let me look at you. Dear Joe!

Duveen (*overcome, lights his cigar, inhales, exhales, emotionally*) Yes, well, who knows – who ever knows – But the thing is, Mary – get well, my dear. And out of this country as quickly as you can, until it's safe again. That's what you must do. All of you. (*Goes to case, picks it up, picks up walking stick.*) Miss Mariano. (*Takes her hand, kisses it.*) I wish I'd had something more – appropriate – to offer.

Nicky It was kind of you to think of me.

Duveen looks at BB. BB lifts his arms for a hug, sardonically.

Duveen May your soul find peace, BB.

BB Car. Train. Boat. Now.

Duveen (*laughs*) You're right, I must hurry, hurry – (*Flourishes his cigar, goes out in a cloud of smoke. Sound of his laughter.*)

BB I spent the whole evening giving him nothing, nothing, at the end he had got nothing from me, nothing, and yet he departs in triumph because the bribe he was giving to one of my women was snatched from his hand by the other! You humiliated me, both of you!

Mary Think what he'd have done if the Swede had been here, too. And still remained a gentleman.

BB (*turns to Mary*) How could you?

Mary (*raises a hand*) Nicky wishes to speak, I believe. My dear?

Nicky Anything I did for him I was only doing for you. You know perfectly well you would have wanted me to open the door for him tonight, you know you would, but you'd have been too proud to say so –

BB How could you – how could you take things from him! Jewellery! Brooches! What else has he given you?

Nicky It's Joe's nature not to trust anyone he isn't bribing, you said so yourself.

BB An occasional cheque – even a little salary, as a retainer for your work as a – an intermediary I might understand. But things to wear – to wear in front of me! From him!

Mary Why shouldn't she? You never give her anything pretty to put on herself any more. She's been your mistress so long you've stopped noticing how much she loves things like that, and what with spying for him so she could spy for you, and going to bed with you every night and putting up with your Swede in the afternoons while being decent and kind to your old wife in the evenings and being your secretary in the mornings on top of it all, I'd say she earned her brooch, she's slaved for it, and she has a right to it, yes, my dear, you have!

BB But she hasn't got it, has she? You've got it.

Mary No, I haven't. Joe's got it. I slipped it into his pocket while he was giving me a hug – one of his own tricks. But it belongs to you, Nicky, go and catch him. Say I said you must have it, must! Or pick his pocket, with my blessing, my dear, whatever you like.

Nicky I'd rather see you back to bed. You're feverish – and you have to keep strong for Karin and little Roger, remember.

Mary She won't be coming. I shall write in the morning, to stop her. It's become too dangerous, you heard Joe, there's to be a war and she'll be glad of the excuse not to come. She's never made to feel welcome, she's made to feel like a beggar. No. Not beggar. I'd forgotten. Beggars are made welcome here, in this house of I Tatti – unless they have something valuable to offer, of course – now, leave me with my husband, please, there's a good girl.

Nicky goes out. There is a pause.
Mary goes to the decanter, pours herself a glass of grappa.

BB That's grappa. It'll harm your stomach, where most of your problems are.

Mary Oh no, my dear – (*with a laugh*) – no, I don't think that's where most of my problems are. (*Takes a gulp, flinches, puts the glass down.*) It is one thing to refuse money for telling the truth. Or to take money for lying. But to lie for nothing – Why?

BB Perhaps because I believe it will do me the world of good.

Mary Your reputation, you mean? It's too late. As Joe probably told you, you already have a reputation for dishonesty. You can't change that with another lie. Not even a profitless one. (*Studies him.*) It won't take you back to what you once were.

BB To what I never was. But might have been if I hadn't met you.

Mary Ah. I corrupted you, did I? Along with Joe, and your Harvard patrons and patronesses, and Nicky too, probably – everyone who ever helped you, admired you, loved you – corrupted you. (*Laughs, nods.*)

BB There is a difference between you and the others.

Mary Yes. The others used you, or let you use them, which is often the same thing. I loved you earliest, understood you first and still understand you best. I founded you. I have been your anchor.

BB No. You founded a lie, and then anchored me to it.

Mary Which particular lie among so many – oh, of course, your Gospels, they've been in your wind for a while, I've noticed. Well, my dear, the truth is that you were incapable of writing them yourself, you were waiting for someone to write them for you. If it hadn't been me it would have been someone else, almost certainly a woman – a wife, probably, for all that annotating and indexing, rather like sewing and knitting, that part of it, the higher knitting and sewing. So it would have had to have been a wife, yes, a very clever wife, just like me, performing a higher wifely duty, just as I did, with whom you would one day be having, or have had, or be about to have, just this conversation. From time to time you've been pleased to have your name on them. And proud. But you're perfectly entitled to disown them – why don't you disown them, BB, if you feel shamed by them?

BB It would be like trying to disown my own grave. The corpses of the best from here and here –

Makes gesture to head and heart. Mary mimics him as he does it.

– are mine, undeniably mine, – I can only pray that their spirit has somehow survived the clods of prose you've shovelled – shovelled – shovelled – shovelled – (*Gestures viciously.*)

Mary Well, now you've buried the past, tell me what you propose for the future. I need to know what to expect for the rest of my life.

BB What the rest of us have to expect, of course. Whatever the future brings.

Mary And my family, my family?

BB I am your family, family. Oh, you mean your natural family.

Mary The family I left for your sake, the family that I gave birth to, cared for, and forsook for – for – (*Gestures at him.*)

BB Ah, the family you *abandoned*. Ah, yes, well, they will have to make their way in life unencumbered by obligations to me. And we'll try not to leave any outstanding debts. With luck, all we have to do is to tighten our belts until the war comes and wipes the slate clean. (*Laughs.*) Think of it, my dear. No history, no past, no art, no provenance, no debts, no Jews, no I Tatti – a new age for new men, free men, slate-wipers, clean-sweepers. (*nodding almost triumphantly*) They will make the world for your grandchildren to inhabit. So what does it matter, a few lies or a few truths in the attribution of a Giorgione or a Titian, one's as good as the other when there's nobody left to look at them, just the duck and Hitler and the new barbarians, who'll make bonfires of them, along with all the books – Sophocles, Aeschylus, Plato, Titian, Giorgione, Leonardo –

Mary runs at him, slaps him.

Mary (*slapping*) Don't smile when you say things like that, don't grin your old man's grin when you say things like that, don't. Don't, don't you dare to say things like that –!

BB at first stands stock still, receiving Mary's slaps, then catches her hands. They stand staring at each other.

BB I didn't mean to grin. I'm not grinning inside. Come – let's sit down. (*leading her by the hand*)

Mary No. No, I don't want to – I don't want to –

BB Yes, you do.

Mary I don't.

Mary allows herself to be led. BB pushes her gently onto the sofa.

Mary (*struggles to rise*) I don't, I don't, I don't –

BB holds her down. Mary subsides. BB sits beside her. There is a pause.

You noticed the cigar – how he lit it, flourished it?

BB Yes.

Mary His usual salute of a triumph. So he must have got something he wanted.

BB As I said just a few minutes ago. The sight of me being humiliated by my women.

Mary Joe isn't petty. He might have enjoyed that, but he wouldn't have celebrated it with a flourish of his cigar. Well?

BB Well. It's true that there is something – yes, something I haven't understood. Of course that's the problem with Joe, you assume there must be a motive within the motive. The fact is, my dear, he didn't get what he came for and I am no longer on his payroll. I'm – I'm –

Mary You can say it. You're a free man, at last.

BB Well, free of Joe, at least.

Mary (*after a little pause*) Perhaps that's what he wanted.

BB For me to be free of him? (*Laughs. Stops.*) Oh. You mean he wanted to be free of me. I see. But why?

Mary says nothing.

Oh. (*Nods.*) Yes. My reputation. Which is – as you said. And he said. And will no doubt get worse, until it becomes positively unfair, eh?

Little pause.

Well, if you're right – at least our final row wasn't about money.

Mary Perhaps it was about money as well. Your insisting on sticking by Titian for *The Adoration* – well, my dear, if you can make that mistake, how many others have you made? All your attributions will become questionable. Joe can use them as he wishes – Yes, yes, the great Berenson himself, the great and irrefutable Bernard Berenson, it turns out he can't tell a – a –

BB A Titian from a Giorgione.

Mary Well, can you?

BB I don't know. But it is now my view – my view – for what it is now worth – that *The Adoration of the Shepherds* was probably mostly painted by Giorgione. And that some further work was probably done on it by his pupil, Titian. Or it may have been the other way round. (*There is a little pause.*) I shall write something to that effect at some time in the future. What do you say to that?

Mary I say that it is faultless.

BB He says – he says he's dying. That he has only three months to live.

Mary Oh!

BB But he was still bargaining when he said it. He made me look into his eyes – they weren't good. But on the other hand he hugged you like a wrestler –

Mary You had better know that I shall never leave I Tatti, BB. I haven't the strength. If this war comes, you will have to go. You're a Jew. You won't be safe here. But I will stay and protect it. I will protect it for as long as I – (*Gestures.*)

BB Whatever the future I promise you we will find enough for those you love. Those others you also love.

Mary (*nods*) I don't doubt you, thank you, but my dear – you were right about the grappa. It was very foolish of me. I must get to bed. Back to bed.

BB I'll take you. (*Rises, holds out his hand to help her up.*)

Mary No, no. Nicky does it, I want Nicky.

BB (*goes to the door*) Nicky! Nicky! Can you come, please!

Mary meanwhile, has risen, is standing, one hand on her stomach, in pain. BB goes to her anxiously, hovers, goes back to the door.

Nicky! Hurry, please! (*Goes back to her.*) Don't you think you'd better let me – I don't know where she is.

Mary She'll be here. She's always here.

BB is about to go back to the door. Nicky enters, goes to Mary. Mary gives Nicky her arm.

And did you catch him, and get your brooch?

Nicky No, he'd already gone. (*helping her*) So I went to my room and cried instead.

Mary I don't believe you. Do you believe her?

BB (*smiles*) It's possible. Anything's possible with women. They have no shame.

Mary What would we need it for? (*to Nicky, as they go off*) Well, my dear, let's hope for the best for tomorrow, let's hope that at least the Swede is back.

BB watches them go off. Sound of their voices, laughter receding. Goes to his desk. Tries to concentrate. Faintly, the sounds of war.

BB hunches himself, as if the sounds are internal, goes to sofa, sits. Closes his eyes, wills concentration.

BB Yes, because one can't see their faces! (*Laughs almost childishly.*) Isn't it ridiculous, that one never remembers that? And yet one should, because that's how it brings the eye – the whole eye – to Mary, Joseph and the baby – just as you'd do it on a stage, a stage grouping, really, as elementary as that – crude almost, until the eye goes beyond, to the boys under the tree, beyond them to the church, then beyond to the mountains, the clouds. Now I've said it I shall remember it whenever needed – (*Little pause.*) – It is needed now.

Sounds of war louder and louder.

Lights.

Curtain.